ME vs HER

TAMI WOODEN

ME Vs Her
Copyright © 2024 by Tami Wooden.

All rights reserved. No part of this book may be reproduced in any form or by any electronic or mechanical means, including information storage and retrieval systems, without permission in writing from the publisher, except by reviewers, who may quote brief passages in a review.

This publication contains the opinions and ideas of its author. It is intended to provide helpful and informative material on the subjects addressed in the publication. The author and publisher specifically disclaim all responsibility for any liability, loss, or risk, personal or otherwise, which is incurred as a consequence, directly or indirectly, of the use and application of any of the contents of this book.

MILTON & HUGO L.L.C.
4407 Park Ave., Suite 5
Union City, NJ 07087, USA

Website: *www. miltonandhugo.com*
Hotline: *1- 888-778-0033*
Email: *info@miltonandhugo.com*

Ordering Information:
Quantity sales. Special discounts are available on quantity purchases by corporations, associations, and others. For details, contact the publisher at the address above.

Library of Congress Control Number:		IN-PROCESS	
ISBN-13:	979-8-89285-015-5	[Paperback Edition]
	979-8-89285-016-2	[Digital Edition]

Rev. date: 01/12/2024

June 2017
Time: 10:13 P.M.
Theme: Tired of Future!
Song: B2K. Bun Bump
Mood: nothing

Every day I wake up, it's the same walls, the same drawing, the same color, when the sun shines, it's so bright & full of life, it's brightens up the world & puts smiles on people faces, when I get ready to step out into the world it's full of noise, buses driving back and forth, cars are driving up and down the block, kids going to school, toddlers are going to daycare, adults are going to work. That's half the world we live in today. The opposite of the world is homeless, drop-outs, female teen pregnancy, drug dealers, in and out of jail, drug addicts, prostitutes, killers, spreading diseases, an average future, husband + wife kids & house, good jobs, good schools, no distractions. Why isn't it more like a normal future?

June 2017
Time: 10:13 P.M.
Mood: empty
Theme: fairy tale
Song: Migo-All ass

The more I see reality shows the more I think to myself. Could life really be like this, parting, sharing secrets, jealousy, betrayed frenemies? Wow that's very interesting, when I watch TV series, it's a whole lot different, who doesn't want the normal fucking life that don't want for nothing, what female doesn't want flowers delivered to her for no reason, what guy don't want a nice warm bath with roses in the tub after a long days of work, that holds no secrets, who is in truly deeply in love & the sex is good, tell each other that you can't live without them, do for each other.... "Happiness" that's all that counts? Brag to your friends, family, co-workers, neighbors, go to sleep every night knowing your waking up to a smile, who wouldn't want that, no sadness, no heart aches, no depression, no weight loss, no crying, to bad this is not a normal life that we live in, you can only

Wish it, or change your lifestyle to make it happen. The perfect guy: no rep sheet, good career, Have a good relationship with his parents good credit, no outside kids, treat women with respect every women's golden ticket...right??? As far as the perfect women: Perfect body, pretty without the make-up, long natural hair, pretty feet, no kids, cat walk, has a relationship with her father, cooks well, makes sacrifices if she has to be independent. Every man's dream right?? Why can't the whole world be like this, everybody gets along, everybody's Happy. Not in today's world, save it for the movies, TV shows, and Hollywood, one day that day will come and instead of watching it on TV, it will be a reality, the money, fame, royalty, the power,

July 2017
Time: 12:16 A.M.
Mood: Deep thought
Song: Cardi B-I like it
Theme: Six feet under

The more they show the different ways you can die the more I think to myself, this could be me one day. How can I defend my child from being attack from a jealous boyfriend, child predator, killer, jealous friends, violence is getting more stronger every day, every day I say to my self is he going to smack me, push me down, throw things, scream violent words at me, ball his fist up at me and start swinging, I fear for my life, she sees it all the time. The day I decide to stop defending my self is the day I say my last good byes to her and the world. The only thing I could do is pray for is that she don't fall in love with an addict. They will hurt you the most. When I'm gone, who is going to pick up where I left off, will she be well taken care of or will she be left stranded to defend for herself. She is the only person I have left to love, please stay on the right direction, make me proud of you. Don't let me down!!!

July 2017
Time: 4:17 P.M
Theme: no life
Mood: mute
Song: Doin 2 Much -
Money baggy o

No friends to play with, no buddies to talk to, no family to vent with, Quiet as a mouse, no drinks to make, no movies to watch, no make-up to put on, painting nails, doing hair, is no fun at all. Who can live like that for so long??? Trap in a box with limited space to reach out that's not how a normal person live in the real world. I have been forgotten is that a good thing, yeah I think so, I like to stay in the shade it's much cooler under there. It's boring sometimes, I'll find someone one day but until then it's just me and you. I love every bit of it. The ones that are close to me, we don't have anything in common, why is that, we grow so fast that we lost track of time, we grew apart no coming back to it, I can't miss what I never had. U.N.I.T.Y.

Aug. 2017
5:30 P.M.
Theme: Home free
Mood: bored
Song: Cake - Trey song 2

Ok so the last time we talk I was in my zone, today I'm feeling older, this is the last month of the summer, kids are going back to school, hopefully mines will be there too. She getting so big and learning so fast I'm trying to keep up thank god I have some help if I get lost but if not she still have 2 more years for normal school to start I'ma be prepared, I'm just hoping that the fall and winter don't give me a lot of problems, I was looking forward into going to the beach but it never happened, our summer wasn't totally boring we had some fun out the deal. Football season is here, new reality TV shows are coming out in so much more, if anything changes until then I will let you know, so far so good. Let's try and keep it that way

Nov 2017
Time: 1:30 P.M,
Mood: Strong
Theme: Helpless
Song: That's my BF

To many people tell me everyday I'm too nice, sweet, soft, weak, get tough, weak-minded, quiet...All my life I thought I was more than that. Am I really all these things people say that I am? Yes I feel lonely all the time, but when I open my eyes I only see one person...me. If I died today, the only good thing I could say about myself is that I left this world right. I've helped a lot of people in my lifetime, but they never returned the favor, they just laughed, shut me up, ignored me, they turned their back on me. So yes I'm all the names they say I am. When I reached for help I realized that it was too late so I gave up. That made me selfish, bitter, angry, but now that I'm older, I was never meant to be a violent, cruel person, I was born to be a lover. I'll take that anyday.

Dec 2017
Time: 5:05 P.M.
Mood: lost
Theme: happiness
Song: Picture perfect-
Trey Song 2

Three years without being myself is not a happy feeling, it's draining me to death, I'm used to being touch in all the right places, kissed in all the soft places, lick in all the happy places, I don't have that anymore, smile all the time "healthy"...We been together so long what is left?? I would love to get that back, but by who?? I'm a mother now I still deserve a little smile, he don't give it to me, should I give up and let me be miserable and let him smile all the time, sure why not, it's been going on this long and he seems not to care about it, so what am I'm supposed to do?? No urge, no feeling numbness, nothing, I'm done, I'm screaming for love, he's deaf, selfish, arrogant, mean, no help here, it's ok, this relationship is burning. I don't need help.

Dec 2017
Time: 2:17 P.M.
Mood: Chilling
Theme: New Chapter
Song: Get it now

As I spend the last week of the year making my child happy with the gifts that Santa gave her, I realize that me and her are the same person and we made it through this year without any health problems, concerns, hungry or homeless. I completed some goals, lovely is in school she doing good, I'm going to get rid of some old things that I don't wear anymore by donating them, made some new friends paying off my debts, some great love ones died but never forgotten, Holli is out of jail, citozz has a good job he is a supervisor for the turnpike, pop enjoying his second home at the stand, this year was very interesting, a lot of fun, drama, crazy, parting, scary things happened but that's a part of life, but one thing I am thankful for nobody in my inner circle pass away for the future, let's keep it that way.

HAPPY NEW YEAR!!

Jan 2018
Time: 11:05 A.M.
Song: Work - Rihanna
Theme: Progress
Mood: Old times

So I'm already in the third week of January and it's been very busy, today is my home girl birthday and we are going to have some fun, we reconnected with some of our family from our old block I really miss them and now that their back in our lives they won't leave me again, as far as me I'm trying to learn more and different things, my brother is starting a company called the black house and I want his dream to come true I support him to the fullest, lovely is still doing good and going to school. I am having bad dreams of dying or getting killed even though I wake myself up out of them. What do they mean? I just wanna grow old, my dad is 62 and still look good, I can't wait til spring gets here, this cold air is in the way.

Feb 2018
Time: 8:24 A.M.
Mood: lit
Theme: GO E.A.G.L.E.S.EAGLES!!!EAGLES!!!
Song: Freaky Friday-Chris Brown

The eagles HAVE WON the Superbowl, I'm so proud of them, they beat my team he New England Patriots, we are going to the Parade and have fun, the time is here and I'm not missing it for the world. Me and Holli got the Black House enterprise on the map now so all we got to do is get the properties and we good to go, the city is lit rite now but on their best behaviors so that's a good thing. I believed in the mind that the eagles were making all the way and they did. It's going be cold but I'm gonna bundle up. I just can't wait. I'm so excited, now after this moment it's back to basketball no more underdogs now, we the champs.

Part 2

We went down to the Parade and it was Lit. I couldn't believe how many people came out and showed Love, I met a lot of people from a different parts of the city, I had so much fun, and the eagles fans...they came in all different shapes and colors, it was a moment I won't forget, me, lovely, Diamond world and Ms. Stacey, we all got split up, but and couldn't find each other but we all got home safe, all the Philly fans did a good job by not doing any bad things to mess up the moment, that speech that the Players and the coaches did was unreal, we was dancing and moving with the crow, moral of the story is that I had a ball and I can't wait to do it again.

Feb 2018
Time: 5:40 P.M
Theme: Tired
Songs: Trey - chill
Mood: Chilled

So now that me and Holli have the black house on black and white it's time to get to business, but since I don't have my degree in anything, I'm a give my ideas and we hire the brainy acts to put it together for me and trust me they will get the credit but I'll be learning as well, the spring time is creeping up soon, that's my baby birthday she will be turning 4 I'm so Proud of her, she learning new things every day, I can't get enough of her I can't wait till real school that's when the real fun begin. I'm gaining some pounds I added peanut butter to my diet, hopefully I can keep it and some.

March 2018
Time: 5:5 P.M
Mood: Peaceful
Theme: Matter of Time
Song: Plies rock

The summer is almost here and I can't wait, the kids be out of school, the black house will be making some money, planning some summer trips, meeting new people and enjoying the sun, new TV shows are coming on, I love the summer because I don't have to wear a jacket, more PPI are out, Penns landing is always popping and who don't like free concerts down at the Ben Franklin Parkway, so now I'm a have to rearrange my dressers drawers with summer clothes but that's cool cause summer and spring are my two favorite season throughout the year.

July 2018
Time: 11:00 pm
Mood: Pissed
Theme: Motherhood
Song: Contagious

Yes I am a 28-year-old mother that has one child that is 4, she doesn't disrespect adults, curse, talk back, act grown, listen to grown PPl talk etc. This pussy told me that I allow her to do whatever she wants and she gonna run over top of me and when she gets older she gonna raise her hands up at me...W.T.F, first of all she gets treated too good to be on that type of level, why would he even wish that on me, kids that be hitting and bullying their parents are the ones that be getting, no attention at home, no love, not cared for, no fathers in their live...etc. She has all that in her life. Even though she's still little right now, I have a long way to go and I hope to live long enough to see it.

Aug 2017
Time: 5:13 P.M.
Mood: Focused
Theme: End of Summer
Song: B.I.D-Tory
Lanez

Summertime is over, back to school kids go, so let's c?? The stand got shut down, we knock it down, the house almost got foreclosure due to a back balance, pop got accepted for home care, Mellah got lock up for being drunk in Norristown, "Tish" she M.I.A. We went swimming, took lovely to the please touch museum, and we went to a company BBQ. I met some interesting people along the way, Holli got promoted to be a trash truck driver, pre-season had started with the eagles, a dollar tree had opened up around the corner so that's love. I think my summer was ok, it could have been a little better but that's ok I'ma c what fall brings to the table, hopefully a little calmer, I'll keep you posted!!

Sept 2017
Time: 2:56 P.M.
Song: Help me help
You - Logan Paul
Theme: fall
Mood: irritated

Now that fall is here lovely is doing good in school, she learning a lot more every day, wentz won his first game back against the colts, I work for Ameri best, I go see my therapist every Monday, Rasheed is not improving at all, we fixing the house up, me lovely and vest went to go see a play called "Christmas cantata" and it was very beautiful, I was surprise by how many people went, I need a new life just me and lovely nobody else, peace and quiet, once I figure out a plane to get it there's no turning back.

Oct 2017
Time: 12:27 P.M.
Song: girl like you
Theme: confused about this country??
Mood: Nervous

They've been talking about this guy sending packages to random democrats and now that they found him, A Jewish church gets shot up, then after that a plane malfunctions and goes down, no one survives. What the hell is going on?? Within 3 days all these things are happening.. why?? The election is coming up in a few days, we as a country need to make some changes my heart goes out to those families it's so sad to see this happen to innocent people, After I learned about this Website called gab, it's just tells me that it's just going to get worst, as far as me ima move forward and love my life.

Nov 17
Time: 1:07 P.M.
Song: Jefe - Meek
Mood: calm
Theme: Who knows

Okay, so we reaching the end of the year, we went thru a lot as a family but we still hanging in there, I have a job so far, Rasheed no longer work for Zak, the sneaker shoe had shut down and moved to south street "So they say." He got a new gig now, I guess 5 days a week, that's good, he's learning and doing something at the same time...let's see how long this last, Ill enjoy the peace for now,, lovely was the little mermaid for Halloween, she looked really pretty. It's a lot of shooting in the area lately I don't know what's going on but it's a lot of anger build up on the streets and its taking the best out of them now that it's starting to get cold the violence will calm down "hopefully"

Date: Nov 2018
Time: 1:07 P.M.
Song: 1:45 - Kirko
Theme: Election
Mood: Good

Democrats won!!

So the election is over and now that we as democrats have some power, no more bowling down to the trump, so starting 2019 we show have a fresh start for the year. Now that that's over another mass shooting at a California, a bar full of college students, the black house got the approval for the new newsstand and so let's see how this new project is going to turn out, can we just get thru the rest of this year without anymore madness and just enjoy the Holidays that are coming up.

Nov 2018
Time: 1:13 P.M.
Mood: Happy
Song: Bed - Nicki Minaj
Theme: family

Thanksgiving just left and it all went well, me and my mother-in-law did all the cooking and everybody loved it, the kids had fun on they days off, I enjoyed my friend that came over me and Rasheed did some early shopping for Christmas, the eagles beat the giants so they still have a fighting chance for the play offs the sixers are doing good with their new help jimmy butler. I'm taking care of myself a little more than I once was before (thanks to a little bit of help) one more month to go and it's over for this year overall all I enjoyed it, meet new people, and reunited with old people, let the countdown begins ☺

Jan 2019
Time: 7:30 A.M
Song: Fr - wiz
Theme: New Events
Mood: Good

The major holidays are over and how it's time for a new beginning, rearranging the house, getting rid of the old and bringing in the new, keeping the low and negative people away from me. We still have our jobs, the Eagles are winning their games since they have Foles back and Wenz is injured. We have to beat the Saints, but if not they still made it to the playoffs, B2K is having a reunion tour this year and I'm going. I'm so excited ima have fun, Lovely is getting big and using big word, the family is doing good, Nae-Nae is pregnant, I'm happy for her Ziana will be a big sister, her due date is August 14. I gained 5 pounds since Kira been here -97-102 thanks Kira - keep feeding me. ☺

Jan 2019
Mood: Shocking
Time: 9:34 A.M.
Song - top 10 - Trey Songz
Theme: God's work

All last week my sister been going thru it with her boyfriend she was 11 weeks, he cause her so much pain by bringing girls in her house having sex with them in her bed, just being, physical, mentally abusive to her and by doing all that stress her out and she lost the baby, blood everywhere, I've never experienced anything like this before, so when they tell you to don't stress during pregnancy, that shit is really true. She was so happy about this baby and for this boy to take it away from her like that is so cruel and evil, he was an asshole anyway so imma take it as god said I refuse to let you have a dead-beat as a baby father. So after she recover she gonna bounce back like this never happened cause she a fighter and I got faith in her and besides she got me ☺

Feb 2019
Time: 8:28 A.M.
Mood: Ok
Song: The dream -
Lemon lean
Theme: Victory

Since the month started Mellah came out of jail, she receive her case money from her mom, Patriots have won the super bowl, it took them a long time to do it but they Pulled it off, nae feels a lot better and she looks much better now that she left skinny-mini alone. V day is in 3 days, the government has opened back up for 3 weeks so I dad my taxes, once I pay my student loans off, I'll feel so much better. My girl Asha be coming over and spend some time with me, we have a couple of week til winter is over,

March 2019
Time: 2:03 P.M.
Mood: fear
Song: Chris Brown
Wishing
Theme: Hopeless place

Everyday I live in fear.. why?? I don't have enemies...do I?? It's so scary in this world now days you don't know what to look out for.. why do I feel like the days I walk up to, is the same days I die too. I'm not happy at all, I feel sad every day, I'll try and find things that are distractive but they don't last long, will I ever be happy the way I would like to be?? Will anybody ever figure me out? I'm not hard to put together. I'm worth more than pleasure (I thought) I guess not (I'll take that) I love the person I've become, I'm glad to put smiles on people faces and rejuvenate their day. That's the darkness that gonna end my life.

May 2019
Time: 10:05 A.M.
Song: Like a porn
Star: August Alsina
Mood: tired
Theme: Love Lost

LOVELY MINES

There's been a lot going on this last month, a lot of drama, screaming, hating jealous people around me, why I don't know but it's driving me crazy, the concert was fun, & hopefully I can go to more like that, one more month for school and it's over. I be so stress out just be wanting to run away and stay away from everybody, the world is warming up and I'm going to enjoy every bit of it, mother's day is coming up am I'm going to get something besides balloons and a card, I think not, that's ok, just because I know that is all I'm worth them, how do I know, cause that the same pattern ever since we meet, nothing more, nothing less.

June 2019
Time: 9:56 A.M.
Mood: Relax
Song: Pnb rock-coupe
Theme: school's out

Tomorrow is the last day of school for Lovely, I'm so proud of her, she went 2 years without one Phone call saying she did something that she wasn't supposed to do. She is growing so fast and learning so much. She is so excited about the new school. I'm also proud of her teachers for taking their time with her. I enjoyed these 2 years and now I'm going to try and enjoy the summer and get ready for real school.

Date: July 2019
Time: 2:51 P.M.
Mood: Bored
Song: Cardi B press
Theme: New Edition

So since the last time we spoke Lovely finish pre-school, now that schools is out, this dum-fuck lost his job, still drinking like it's no tomorrow, Holli and Shantae is expecting a baby (think god) more wooden added to the family, her due date is the 9th so now I'm a aunty to a closer niece, we got a car and still didn't do anything fun with it, now he was so hype about it and he all stressing cause he can't keep up with nothing else, he's the license driver but still didn't prove it to me yet. No responsibility yet!! We got the car in May, I'll give it 6 months

Aug. 2019
Time: 10:06 AM
Theme: Drug free
Song - Sammie-
Get right

Extra, Extra Read All about it!!!

So Holli got his baby from the hospital and ever since then it's been downhill from then, Shantae had drugs in her system so DHS had to be involved, the baby had appointment so far and Shantae snap out at both of them, the doctors was so scared that they had to call the case worker and tell her what's going on. So last week the case worker comes out to close the case and this girl runs off wit the baby, so now Holli throws me under the bus by tell the case worker its my fault I let her escape and all this other stuff, so when the cops come he telling them the same thing, but not one time they ask me for my of information or got in trouble for it, cause at the end of the day I didn't sign no paperwork saying I'm going to be responsible for Sharee. He's mad about it. Oh well, his problem, not mine. She was running off before she got pregnant, now he's all stressed out. No baby - no ass - the baby is safe with the aunt or cousin. Who knows, and she got 302 - Dum bitch she knows from right and wrong, the crazy part about it is Sheed has to hear about it every day when he goes to work with him, he telling every body about on the job, outside the job, he telling them about his rape cases and maybe even the lawsuit, he needs to learn how to shut his mouth, his court date is Wednesday for ce-ellie, let's see how that goes.

Aug 2019
Time 12:49 P.M
Theme: One-man Army
Song: Sammie-
Impatient
Mood: Quiet

I ask myself every day when I wake up, please don't let today be a nightmare, some days be good, most days depression, I'm surrounded by evil, sick corrupted, disrespectful, careless problems that I got to see or hear, that's very unfair cause the normal person that I'm am can't take but so much. I think to myself how did it get this bad. The crazy part about it, I share the same blood line, I find many distractions to avoid from getting anywhere near it but it's always find me, as long as it don't involve me or my love bug I Don't Give a fuck!! Keep your problems to yourself. If you put yourself in a tough situation, you need to get yourself out of it.

Aug 2019
Time: 2:01 pm
Song: Sammie-
Truth is...
Mood: Clean

Karma is really something to believe in, how are you a man of god and listen to what he says, but steady talking down on people like you so perfect, you the main devil in this situation, now look the car won't start, your phone won't come on...What the hell...Stop talking shit and think you the man and you know it all. You just an old as creep try na stay young by hanging with the young crowd...you will never be young again so sit ya ass down and read a book and stop being in everybody business cause you're not helping...at all so after he gets the car fix let's see what else karma has in stores for him, hopefully it hits him personally.

Oct 2019
Time: 10:2/2 A.M
Mood: friendly
Theme: Too much pressure
Song: 111 baby
Oh okay

Down Hill Spiral!!!

Omg...too much is going on to fast, tree out the program so now pop riding around with her and picking Zay up from school everyday like that's his child and putting other people on the back burner for her, Welfare tells me that I make too much so they cut me and lovely off of medical so now that I have medical thur my job I have to pay for lovely...that's cool I need her healthy, but that also means that imma have to switch programs cause they only take mediaid..that sucks.. I guess that cool no more welfare in my life☐Lovely doing good in school she likes her teacher and her friends adore her, so now I have to deal the 6 moths worth of cold air, I just can't let me or Lovely get sick, Sheed still have his job so far so that's good nae ex-boyfriend was released from jail so now she scared for her life.

Oct 2019
Time: 3:25 P.M
Mood: friendly
Song: Saweetie - My Type

Power House Weekend

I'm so excited for this weekend Ima get to see all the Hot artists that came out wit hits all summer long, I needed this because I don't do shit for myself or nobody doesn't do nice things for me. that's fuck up that's cool cause ima keep thinking about myself and lovely, my tickets better be real I get to see my migos in person (omg) me and my squad is gonna have a blast

Part 2

The concert was good we all had a good time the migos was the last performance but they never come out maybe because the money bag wasn't right. The night still ended with a good time.

Oct 2019
Time: 10:56 A.M.
Song: Neyo-Mirror
Theme: unpretty

Pretty face   Pretty mind
Pretty smile   Pretty girlfriend
Pretty Attitude   Pretty sister
Pretty walk   Pretty skin
Pretty mom   Pretty soul
Pretty daughter   Pretty Lover

All these things that I've named I wake up everyday believing that it's true but as far as I know it's all a lie, I will never look the same as I did before. I get laugh at every chance I get – no help from nowhere to tell me different, the ones that see differently don't stay around long or they find ways to keep themselves away. All this work for nothing I'm over it. I should just drop dead now who would care besides Lovely. All this confidence that I once had about myself is no longer alive, its eating me up inside, I try and find different distractions to keep my mind off the bad things that have been clouding me but the distractions didn't live up to what I expected it to be so I had to let it go, it wasn't making me feel any better then what I already felt, my life is based on people getting over on one another and don't care who's get hurt in the process. A girl like me with all them traits shouldn't be in a horror story

Nov 2019
Time: 2:18 P.M.
Song: Dani Leigh Lil Babe
Theme: recapping 2018

We in November Christmas is next month and then its New Years...Wow so let's see what have I accomplish up until now... (thinking) staying alive, keeping Lovely out of harm's way, found another job, Lovely had her surgery and that was a success, I got a tooth pulled that will no longer bother me anymore met some new friends along the way we have some New Artists came out with some Hot shit that I'm grooving to, lovely is growing so fast I'm so proud of her. She gets along with her classmates (so far) no major problems with the teacher (I'm doing good as a mom). I'm just glad that I'm here to see it all.

Nov 2019
Time: 3:26 P.M
Song - Haley Smalls
Scared of me

She is something else!!

Smile - got it

Walk - Love it

Style - talking it

Brain - Can't match it

Skin - Radiant

So what's the problem - Everybody wants it, she can't please the world but she's doing her best, it can get tiring at times but she keeps going. Why does she show this side of her (it's to attaching) too hard to break a way, this kind of figure should never be fuck wit (it too hard to handle) in the female rank she is on the top of the list. (Lucky her) that's a lot but oh well (she loves it) for now one day it will end or not (who knows) as long as she is doing her job very well it should be no problem.

Nov 2019
Time: 2:09 P.M
Song: Ty Dolla sigh Surrounded
Theme: Counting Down

This year is almost over Lovely got her first report card (very good) not giving the teacher Mrs. Green any problems, all her friends love her so that's even better, 2020 is slowly approaching do I want to change or do something different – Hell yeah...Please take all the negatives (including people) out my life and never come back...Will that wish come true (who knows) I'm a have to wait and see, I have Patience, the new people that I met (good distraction) but for How long?? I'm immune to being abandoned – it gets tiring sometimes but I'll survive. Any goals that I wanna set myself-keep me and lovely alive during the Mayhem of a city that we live in. She means everything to me.

Nov 2019
Time: 1:30 P.M.
Song-Trey Songz
How could You Forget

Out of control!!

How could you let this Habit go on for sometime now...too long!! it's time to be free from it all, what did you learn...nothing at all because the craving will always gonna be there, just like that the story ends, not yet a new chapter so far, let's see ima take it slow, keep quiet...if I can help it!! All I need is the fall/Winter to hurry up and go so I can enjoy my life again, (dark, cloudy, stormy, windy) (all signs of bad things) I still have my phone didn't lose that yet, thanksgiving is here (thank you god for waking me and lovely up every morning to see each other

Nov 2019
Time: 11:32 A.M'
Song: Doja Cat- Cyber sex

EVIL Lives Here!!!

Father - Husband

Violent aggressive, controlling, demanding show off, Selfish, loquacious, Hypersexual alcoholic.-

Son - Brother

Violent, aggressive, controlling, demanding show off, selfish, loquacious,

Dec 2019
Time: 8:41 A.M.
Song: Pop smoke -
Welcome to the party

Not that much to go!!

So it's a lot going on as we approach a new beginning of a new chapter...So far there will be another millennium tour but this time it won't be the full group B2K...lil fizz and April is dating now so they are no longer be a group so that's cool, I went to the first one and that was good enough for me, if I come up with the money I'm going to the Second one, Pop kept telling tree that he wasn't going take her to work so when he wasn't around she took the keys and ran off with the car for a couple of hours, we let Shantae stay with us until Holli came out until her medicine started wearing off on her so now she going nuts Ant-man labtop goes missing so she had to go.

Pop buddy James no longer works for Einstein, so every chance he gets pop drunk to the point he can't pick people up for work. Nae gets treasure a job, she starts telling the people at the job about her and nae side hustle, for what reason (who knows) Holli still hasn't been released yet (I know he pissed). Being drunk pops knock a whole piece of bumper off the car (smh) I told the car dealer lady I'll give him 6 months until something goes wrong with it...I don't even care anymore I don't drive anyway. I go to work and I get left but not once, twice I was forced to walk home at 2 in the morning, thank god it wasn't cold that day so I was good... but still I shouldn't have to. But it's cool cause the next time it happens I won't be nice, Lovely...Well she just keeps me happy she got 2 awards good report card no phone calls, just awesome and for that she got a puppy, as far as me goes...I'm not where I wanna be in life, health, mentally, physically, emotionally sexually...

like I'm all fucked up, like how did I let this happened, I know how once I let negative energy in my life everything went down hill from there, will I ever be fully happy once again (I'll believe not) but if the day or moment happens I will let you know, now what can I expect when this new year come, more craziness something gonna happen to the car hopefully hollo get out and get to work, get C- Ellie back.

Jan 2020
Time: 4:16 P.M.
Song - Rotimi - in my bed

New Beginning... So they say

So let's see, I let some people go, they showed no interest in coming back, that's cool with me, people better start paying their Phone bill or all lines will get canceled. Eventually ima quit my job and leave people stranded. Our house is still a shelter for people, Sheed is still drinking like it's no tomorrow, Nae is a Pro at driving so I let her take over the wheel... I'm cool Septa is my forever friend unless I need to.... I'm still debating on should I still go to this concert...The house is falling apart even more, this year is gonna be the end for a lot of people. Hopefully I'm one of them...no??? I would liked to see another day but for how long before the sun sets on me I'ma close my eyes and wait until the silence breaks...

Jan 2020
Time: 5:22 P.M.
Song: Rotimi - Love Riddim

We already in the first week of the year and already it starting off messy, trump blowing up the head general of Iran so now they angry and wants pay back so now we have to send all our men that have families to fix or go to war for his fuck up...smh pop still dealing we treasure she got a car (a cab) so far she making money out of it. I still feel unhappy...I haven't Seen Alex in a few months so I'm really going through it. I'm glad my friends pop back up in my life, they are working and maintaining.

Jan 2020
Time: 4:19
Song: Jacqueese - Come get it
Mood: Day off

Ok so as I thought all lost of hope for me and then boom out of the blue my happiness come to save me, but only for the moment, I don't know was it is but when I be having my Solo moment somebody's always listening thank god for that, So, so far we are getting the process along the probation people came out to the house and installed the house arrest box so now we just waiting on the jail to release him

June 2020
Time: 2:52 A.M.
Mood: Embarrassed
Song: Ton Romiyi Loyal

May - June Madness!!

So there is still trouble in the kingdom...Memorial Day, started out like a normal day but end in a ungraceful way, starting with the neighbors threatening people, paying people to do ya dirty work using good people into ya dirty little mind...but once the equal gender confronts you...You balls up...all talk...You making enemies everywhere you go, see, touch, money can't solve everything, god don't like ugly. Georg Floyd was buried safely, the whole wide world protested for his death during this coronavirus they did not care, so after today let's see if there will be anymore

June 2020
Time: 3:27 A.M
Song: Kiss it-Rihanna
Theme: Worthy
Mood: unsure

I wake up everyday and think to myself, I'm so glad to see my daughter's face, then I look at her dad and think can I have made this angel with somebody else, of course not...So why do I feel like it's not enough for me?? don't get me wrong I am very loved by many ppl because of who I am, but what is missing is I'm not being loved the way I need to be, not by money, conversating, disrespect, lies, abandonment, addictions, Real Love by clear minded people that knows what they want out of life, drama free, strong minded, protector, reliable, Pretty smile, she is all in one, so what's the problem, she won't sit still until that one curve trips her fleet....I'll wait patiently, I believe in me, like I was been saying, everybody shake hands with everyone that's in the higher power rank, starting with trump on down, all this chaos that be going on while I'm at work, it never happens when I'm here. me chilling upstairs, why does he think he can have control over women, you're not the boss of no one you can't fight...All Bark!!

June 2020
Time 1:21 A.M.
Mood: curious
Song: Lildurk- Gucci
Theme: New Beginnings

So there's a lot of new development going on without anyone talking about it, Mr. President brought an engagement ring (black diamond) at that☐the day he propose to her I hope I'm there to see her answer, will she say yes or no??? If she say yes it's because she is thinking for the further and she can use the money to get away and never come back (I see this turning into something that no female has to go through) If she says no she is the smartest women he's been with, 2 month pregnant, (why, why, why) new stepdad, new stepmom, I don't think they can handle the pressure that comes with it.

June 2020
Time: 3:45 A.M.
Song: King von- Took her to theo
Theme: Any means Necessary.

It is getting down to the wire, the president wants the crew to get out the black house he calling the cops, getting retraining orders, pop got nae catching Uber and lyfts home (like what) All because Ciani is not holding up her part of the bargain, they all supposed to be leaving on the 1st but the president wants them out now (I'm exhausted) with this whole thing. Now I really hope they get their new apartment on the 1st cause I'll hate to see the kids on street but Mr. President doesn't care, we won't stop until they are removed and the locks are changed. Black House Power!

Aug 2020
Time: 1:19 A.M.
Song: Beyonce- Black Parade
Theme: no type

So far the last month it's been the same old stupid evil, unnecessary, bullshit drama for no reason, father's day weekend in the mist of kicking nae and her crew out the black house, he either paid somebody or paid Ms. Regina to say that mid, destiny and sweet pea went over to change the locks pepper spray her and push her in the closet and threw her phone in the toilet (so he come up with this story to get them lock up for doing that) apparently it worked cause destiny was the first to get caught (that whole story didn't sit right wit me so I just listened) he deserved every bad thing that's coming to him (it makes me sick to my stomach knowing what I know about him) when that day comes ima turn the other way.

Aug 2020
Time: 6:54 P.M
Song: Popsmoke Hello
Theme: Summer Wrap up

I'm still working (both jobs) the summer is slowly ending – no fireworks, no parades no swimming (private owned only) we did go to A/C twice (Caesar, Ballys) they both was nice and comfortable, lovely she had a ball both trips, as the fall enters I'm looking for individually space (me and my 2 amigos) I've fill out some apps and requested touring times and dates (so let's see how it goes) if I get approve (omg baby) I'll just hope for the best (if not, I'll keep trying)

Aug 2020
Time: 6:25 A.M
Song: Pop Smoke Woo
Theme: The clash of the titans

Virgo War!!

Boy I'll tell you if anybody pick this book up (man o man) so finally the 2 Virgo have finally separated themselves apart and it's for a long time (this girl done stabbed her brother right above his chest) to the point he could of died now he laid up in the hospital internal bleeding from one of his main artery, so now he all stitched up and this girl going down for violating probation and for attempt-murder (smh), lovely could of been fatherless, I told them to stay away from each other (being to close can get you hurt or killed) we won't be seeing Mellah for a while (damn shame)

Sept 2020
Time: 11:33 P.M
Song: Don't Rush

FALL Has Begun!!

So the COVID-19 is still floating around online schooling has begin, everybody is doing well and fine, in the progress of getting my own peace of mine, my daughter Love-bug (omg) if she ain't a tough cookie then I don't know what to call it... She seen, heard, and been through it all, that's my baby, she loves the shit out of her dad (me on the other hand don't feel that way) I won't take that from her, Sheed turned another year (yay for him) this online thing is not working for me, they need one on one teaching, let's see How this thing go and How many parents or students are taking this online class serious they can't fail nobody...Right???

Sept 2020
Time: 1:37 P.M.
Song: Popsmoke-
Rock the boat

Never Ending Story

So after destiny leaves, she comes back to get her stuff, now she's in another robbery (smh) she flips the script and get an restrainer order against him and now it's withholding him to get c-ellie back (what are you doing Holli) back to square one, Do he really want to go to jail again our whole lives can change in one month, why can't you just be calm and humble (stay the fuck still) Sheed back in the hospital cause he was getting swelling around the wound, he wound up staying due to his yellow eyes, inflammation in the liver next step. "Death" ima stop drinking... We will see...

Sept 2020
Time: 2:32 P.M
Song: Gonna-Nasty girl
Theme: Moving on up

So school has started up online and it doing ok so far. I have to wake up in the morning and get her ready, the other kids look like they wanna go back to bed. I had put a deposit down for the new apartment, hopefully it gonna be on Spencer St. but if not Mervine it is...next to Kevin and Ms. Tammy, Tree had her baby, she told Holl: it wasn't pops; she got the baby taken and now she's in the system, Rasheed liver is going down Hill who knows how much time he has if he doesn't fix this problem, "love bug" she is doing good growing up, learning fast. I love her so much, I see myself in her every day, I wish my mom could see this.

Oct 2020
Time: 3:52 A.M
Song: Throat baby
Theme: On the Run

I know I haven't been keeping up all month, but I'm here now so let me update you. Love bug is still doing online school work, I'll be at my new apartment in no time nae got a new car, Sheed bang up Holli Lincoln so he had to upgrade, so since the dealership was in jersey that cause him to come back a little bit past his curfew and now they tryna lock him up for it...So now him and destiny are on the run...At the same damn time (smh) Pop plotting so bad against him just so he can have the car Mellah and mid still lock up, Sheed just drinking away. All I asked for is to not die in my bed, he just enjoys not going to work, but once this pandemic money runs out, what does he have left, nothing at all. All these holidays are coming up and I don't have the money like I used to so lovely might not even get a Christmas just because I know Ima be having to pay the bills all by myself. He's gonna start some dumb shit while I'm not around and get himself hurt or killed...I'll be waiting. Lovely, she's chilling, growing big, she with her friend for the weekend. I'm so excited about my new place, I'ma make it into a home. I don't have to look at pop face nor hear his giant negative ass mouth. I don't think they gonna keep up the place once they get it fix, if they do, then power to them, uncle Mike and Ms. Ronda had adopted lucky from us, that's cool cause they can have something to remind them of us when we leave, and besides I can't afford cat food at this time so I know she will be taking good care of so no worries on that part. We just have to find another one. This thing with pop and nunu is getting outta control. She runs the show and pops doesn't say nothing, I ask him to do one thing, and she tells him something different. Pop is about to sink like the titanic and when he does,

I'm gonna see it, is his bitch's is gonna bring him back up to afloat?? Fuck no, but not in his eyes (smh) once I cut all tides from him I'll feel better gorgeous she 8 months now, chewing up everything and wanna play all the time, so now that the house is quiet, pop is super happy, telling all the neighbors Holli out the house (Shut the fuck up, you talk too much).

Oct 2020
Time: 11:59 P.M.
Song: Rod wave -
Rag 2 Riches
Theme: fall season

Football Status!!

AFC East

Bills - 4 - 1
Patriots 2 - 2

Dolphins - 2 - 3
Jets - 0 - 5

AFC West

Cheifs - 4 - 1
Raiders - 3 - 2

Broncos - 1 - 3
Chargers - 1 - 4

AFC North

Steelers - 4 - 0
Ravens - 4 - 1

Browns - 4 - 1
Bengals - 1 - 3

AFC South

Titans - 4 - 0
Colts - 3 - 2

Texans - 1 - 4
Jaguars - 1 - 4

NFC East

Cowboys - 2 - 3
Eagles - 1- 3 - 1
Washington - 1 - 4
Giants - 0 - 5

NFC North

Packers - 4 - 1
Bears - 4 - 1
Lions - 1 - 3
Vikings - 1 - 4

NFC West   NFC North

Seahawks - 5 - 0   Saints - 3 - 2
Rams - 4 - 1   Burcaneers - 3 - 2
Cardinals - 3 - 2   Panthers - 3 - 2
49ers - 2 - 3   Falcons - 05

As I look at these scores it looks like COVID 19 is impacting some teams and the rest is doing just fine. Well at least that's what I'm thinking it's a lot of good rookies that playing really good this year to me it feels so different, no real noise in the crowd cardboard people are looking at them, like what the hell, totally awkward, we got a little bit more to go wit this season,

Super Bowl Feb 7 "21"

Brady VS Kansas City

Now this should be a good one mohomes he is making a name for himself and for his team, I'm very proud of both teams making it to the end of the road, now it's god's willing my the best team wins, now after the super bowl is over ima need a new hobby to find on Sunday, the super bowl is hosting in Tampa bay so that dope, if Brady ever retire without me seeing him, just know he was my first and last quarter husband.

Nov 2020
Time: 12:24 P.M
Mood: Relax
Song - Da baby
Carpet burn
Theme: Holiday Weekend

The President Has Fallen!!

For how long?? Who knows, he invested into soo much into this beauty salon, destiny got out, text me and say that the girl Tasha went in her bag and tried to link her card to her cash app and get $100 out her account and it had alerted her phone cause the transaction didn't go thru, her and Sheed goes around to the blackhouse to approach Tasha about it but she denies it, she brings her homie up so they try to get thru the window but Sheed and old head ray was blocking their way, so we called the number that was linked to the card and it's the new girl Makayla that was doing it (smh,W.T.H). She's goes and tells me that Holli tried to rape her, put his hands on her and threatened her and her family, threw her out the car while it's freezing cold, (W.T.F) the same Shit every female said that he did to them, another scared women by his controlling evil ways. Well he is sitting right now, but this time it's with guns and pills, damn shame Holli, you did it to yourself, ima wait patiently and see if he gets bailed or he's a done deal, well so far the girl Tash is holding it down for him "thank god" she can handle that he really needed a sit down he was doing to much and moving to fast, they cracked open the safe and took whatever it was in their, can't wait until I hear his charges, he keep hurting women and now it's caught up to him, if he go up top and get a # he really done, I know for a fact he aint built for that, they might rape his ass, I'm upset that I had to here that shit the way that I did, now that I know that he still up to his old ways, he got home Kitty, " what's the problem"god know everything and now I do too. Everyday I have to live knowing that I have a mental sickness in my family that preys on the weak and valuable. Do you know how sick to my stomach that makes me feel?? And for that god needs to suck this disease out of him...it's not healthy...its burning me the fuck out if god put him away he can't hurt anymore innocent souls, me and the world would be at more peace.

Part 2

Time: 9:45 p.m

So he calls and Sheed talks to him he mad because nobody wouldn't take the charges for him(dum fuck, who would) I thought the girl tyaber did it because he cursed her out the night before but she didn't Makayla did, she didn't waste no time, she took a monster off the streets, he wasn't sharing the wealth anyway so why should I care about anything at the black house, the girl Tasha can have that shit, even sale it, he lived to see the lavished life, now his whole empire have collapse, after he knows the verdict and if and when he get convicted I'm blocking him from our lives, he was no good to us as a family or society it's gonna hurt lovely not to see her uncle for a long time but she will get over it thru time, it's looking real bad for him. I'll keep updated.

Lovely did very good on her report card this year (with mommy help) I can't wait until this year is over so we can both sleep longer. The whole week of thanksgiving, the weather was super nice "now that's a first" the COVID-19 is still killing people by the minute, it got so bad that it had alert everybody phone.

Date: Dec 2020
Time: 8:28 P.m
Song: CJ - Whoopty

Last month of the year!

Lovely is doing good in her school work, my second month in my apartment, gain new friends, Bien is the new president, they found a cure for covid-19 they granted us another stimulus check but trump saying 680 isn't enough (that's an insult to society) $2,000 should be good, the prison system upgraded to tablets now, so now you can see the person, we finally got the steps fixed to the basement, Lucky is at Rhonda house and now we got a new cat black and white, a couple of people had died along the way, Holli and Mellah are doing good, all my main people are still alive and maintaining, we got a new spot light on the new quarterback (Hurts) I received 2 of the 4 leggings that I ordered. The company said that they would replace my money if I don't receive the other too and they better. I'm still working. The crew is cool, they all adore lovely. Hopefully next year's sports season will be better than this one. This covid is still affecting a lot of people and people are still dropping like flies from it so it's very heartbreaking. Thank god this virus hasn't touched me or my loved ones. Lovely is going to enjoy a cheerful Holiday and that is all that counts.

Date: Dec 2020
Time: 11:05 P.M.
Song: Pop Smoke- Diana
Theme: 2020 over

Blessed!!

So glad to be alive, food in my mouth, clothes on my back, roof over my head, no harm to me or lovely, reunited with some childhood friends, gained some friends, met new people, cut the fake people, I've done seen people true colors. The COVID disease is still killing people. The eagles didn't make it to the playoffs

Jan 2020
Time: 4:19
Song: Jacqueese-
Come get it
Mood: Day off

Ok so as I thought all lost of hope for me and then boom out of the blue my happiness comes to save me, but only for the moment, I don't know was it is but when I be having my Solo moment somebody's always listening thank god for that, so so far we are getting the process along the ppl come out to the house and put the box so now we just waiting on the ppl to release him

Jan 2020
Time: 3:20 P.M.
Song - Neyo - One more

Okay, so we are almost at the end of the month and so far we made some progress, Holli is out of jail..."finally" but he still have some cleaning up to do so hopefully this is the last and final time with this court shit, now he go to trial in April I hope the judge and the jury see that she is lying and let this situation go and all of this can be over wit... if not Holli can be looking at some crazy time and his money is gonna go wit him that's cool... he gonna need it, Pop is still on some grimy shit putting pussy over everything karma gonna get his ass back to. I don't want him doing time when he accomplished so much to go right down the drain but if it has to come down to that... long lived Mr. President.

Jan 2020
Time: 4:24 P.M.
Song - Future
Good life
Mood - Under the Weather

Ok so we went around the black house and it's all Jack up...Doors off the handles, the heat is on 100 degrees and they all coupe up in the rooms...WTH...They was blaming it on Hellboy for the mess they made. I told them that they didn't have any home training, they were cool, they didn't get out of line. Holli went back to his job after a long 4 month of lock down, I know they were glad to see him he went to get his physical over and now he just waiting for the HA to approve it (they better not take long) I glad I heard some familiar voices over the weekend so I feel good about that. Lovely doing good in school, she is getting so big and smart at the same time. I love lovely to death

Jan 26 2020
Time: 6:56 P.M.
Song: Khalid-Eleven
Mood: Treglic

Extra, Extra Read All About It!!!

Coby Bryant passed away today due to a helicopter crash...Wow (smh) the fans are going crazy about it, his teammate can't believe it, it just doesn't feel real yet but it is...??? Diamond world Lost my speaker some how while waiting for Rasheed to do his taxes, what a strange day, we still in the first month of the year and shit still didn't change yet I was never a Bryant fan but he was very good at what he did, this is very sad cause one of his daughters had died with him so that's even more painful, I hope no more celebrities die this year, Besides that I'm doing ok Shantae pop back up so they united back together again, pop keep playing these silly games like I won't beat him the fuck cause I will

Feb 2020
Mood: Bored Time: 10:50 A.M
Song - TinaShe - Boss

Last Day for Football

So Andy Reid won his first super bowl in his life I'm proud of him he work very hard for that now Imma need something to watch so now that we had got them stray dogs out the apartment, Nae and ciani stay there now, pop soo hype like he put them in there himself now he wants za to go to the same school that Lovely goes to...like nooo see I have a strange feeling that this summer is gonna come wit a whole lot of problems starting with pop thinking he control everything (it's really pissing me off)

Feb 2020
Time: 3:56 P.M.
Song - Beyonce -
Grown Women
Mood - disappointment

Little Too Hotty!!

So the day was going good - watching King - Kong - Jaws videos from Disney world - then Bam She wants to take the baby - Cellie and Sndreana - from there it went from Shantae wat time is your appointment - 11pm Holli look thru the papers (Smh) Pregnancy papers (Direct violation) She thought she was gonna raise a baby that came from a nut ass nigga oh Hell No!!! We aint having it (out the kingdom for you) thanks for Cellie - WE got her naughty, naughty, naughty, Bad Shantae, that your problem not ours, long lived the 1st Lady...Next

Feb 2020
Time: 12:49 P.M.
Song - Ann Marie
One Mo Time
Mood - Unlove

Love month Meltdown

I go through a lot of emotions for a lot of things, but for what, cause I don't move forward with it, either I wound up hurting myself, making someone else happy or snapping out because I did both it's cool, that's what I'm good at pleasing people...The million dollar question is when will I ever gonna be happy, the way I really wanna be, it don't take much for me...I'm a real simple girl - trust me it won't take long to figure me out and when that person or someone do it's my choice if I want to be stuck with it or not. I've been making some good choices in my life so far so this one shouldn't be a problem.

Feb 2020
Time: 10:06 A.M.
Mood: inspired
Theme: Jealous
Song: Dirty Diana

(I Just Don't understand)

Jealousy - thoughts or feelings of insecurity, fear, concern over a relative lack of possession.

Insecurity - uncertainty or anxiety about oneself - lack of confidence open to danger or threat

Unwanted - no longer desired

Violence - physical force intended to hurt, damage, destructive force

Scorn - the feeling of belief that someone or something is worthless

Now that I just broke down every symptoms that this dumfuck has he fuck up and needs help...Bad

Feb 2020
Time: 11:23 P.M
Song - Different
Mood - Uneven

Valentine's Day Weekend

The whole month of February is considered to be Love and black History month so let's see who got both for this month.

Simple traits that makes me fall in love

1.) Consistency
2.) Ambition
3.) High Sex drive
4.) Non-judgmental
5.) Lover
6.) Self love

History

We in 2020 what history did we continue to follow, none of them, we still having killings, there are still injustice in the world, make America great again, how mix color going to war together, trump over brushing his power in the white house

Feb 2020
Time: 4:10 A.M
Song - Pop Smoke
Christopher walking
Mood: disappointed

Breaking News!!

The rapper pop smoke was found dead in his home Wednesday morning during a home invasion...WTF!!! Yoo bull jus came out and all his music is not, how the fuck and why the fuck did this happened...smh hating ass mother fuckers...R.I.P. Pop on some other type time, he hit somebody mirror so now the transmission is jack up so we put the Honda in the shop, now that we using holli car pop got Holli car slightly hit so now everybody is back to square one...catching septa, I don't care about going to work I would love to stay home and don't do shit they just gonna have to rehire me when the pilot gets out the shop. Oh well

Feb 2020
Time: 10:54 A.M
Song - Ann Marie
Make Love
Mood: good

Drama, Drama, Hear All about it!!

He just don't quit like omg u come out of jail doing the same shit being controlling and thinking he run everything yes that's your apartment but you gave them the key to move in, stop plotting on Mfr's that don't want you they know your habits already dummy, why would they fall for it and besides why would you want something that not even ya type (so you say) this guy is crazy, he better not do nothing crazy to make his ass go back in and this time he won't come out, all he need is to stay focus on the black house and his money and Cellie that's all nothing else. It's a damn shame that we all came from the same bloodline.

Feb 2020
Time: 9:32 A.M.
Song: Perfect Bitch
Mood - Ok

New Season

Winter is almost gone Love bug Birthday is next month the big 6...Wow I'm so proud of her she just every mother could dream of...A major thanks to her dad (built ford tough) school is over in a couple months and I must say once again I judge correctly - good grades as always as far as me nth change - maybe my hair styles and my hair polish, still looking at the same boring people everyday... Where's the fun in that (nowhere) hopefully I'll see some more sunshine as the days get warmer.

MAR 2020
Time: 3:19 PM
Song: Pop Smoke
She got a thing
Mood: warming up

Thank god the major season is over with, we didn't get to much cold and snow this year so that was cool, warm weather is slowly coming but on love - bug birthday it better be saying something I can't wait till the big day tomorrow I'm a have fun, if I didn't go to this one I was gonna be upset, I can't wait to come back and tell you all about it. I got the weekend off so I'ma enjoy myself (hopefully) Larry, Larryanna, and Janice supposed to be coming down also so that's gonna be fun and something different, the car is taking forever to get out the shop but that's the pilot needs a break from pop, he keep getting all these different types of tickets, thank god the Penndot company don't know me yet.

MAR 2020
Time: 10:59 A.M.
Song - Omarion - Can You Hear Me
Mood: quiet

The After Party

The concert was Litty once again, I made it up to the front of the stage and it was crazy everybody was jamming, I'm really glad that sheed didn't make me miss that show. Ashanti was a surprise guest and she killed it 8 more days until Love - bug birthday, Larry and Larryanna had came down to the city. Also they chilled and stayed the night, we slowly up-grading the house. Two days ago a guy got shot right in the head a broad & chew, (8:48 A.M) That's crazy, the guy got caught doe, spring is almost here I'll be 30 with one child, Ms. Green didn't come back yet from having her baby but Ms. Bailey she cool, the kids are not giving her too many problems, hopefully the pilot comes out of the shop, the Lincoln is cool but boring and quiet.

MAR 2020
Time: 12:25 P.M.
Song - young thug
Relationship

Outbreak Alert!!

This CoronaVirus is getting out of control. They shut half the world down because of this man made project, the kids having fun but not the parents, it's a setback for them. I'm not afraid of the virus, it's gonna get whoever it wants, I'm glad my concert happened before this outbreak got worse.

Part 2 outbreak!!

This outbreak is not stopping at all the death toll is over 11,000 people ... that's the fastest death in history within a week the streets are quiet, jobs that are open are moving in slow motion, the supermarts are running out of food, the hospitals are running out of beds, it has gotten so bad the trump has put the whole U.S.A on a curfew because of the Airborne illness Love bug still enjoyed her birthday that all that counts, more famous ppl catching the virus, it's really getting scary, sooner or later the crime rate is gonna get larger and that's not good for older people, I'm not bothered by this situation, it gonna touch who it wants (coronavirus) you will never be forgotten in history - damn shame. A lot of people are going to have a boring birthday (including me) and it's very, very sad.

April 2020
Time: 10:14 A.M.
Song: Rotimi -
Want more

EASter Sunday

So this outbreak is getting workers laid off their jobs, people doing more killing, robing and doing all types of crazy things...the numbers is getting higher, at work we gotta talk to the customer thru a glass, gloves on, mask up...What the hell

April 2020
Time: 11:42 A.M.
Song: Tory Lanez
KLOK

New girl to the Block

So since the first Lady have been removed from the Kingdom for being disloyal the President have found a replacement that came with a package so far everybody is getting along but I'm not to convince that it's gonna stay like that (I know him) I'ma keep falling back and watch the show, now I'm pretty sure she must be thinking (why she being AntiSocial) I believe she has a leak somewhere in her life that's just not fitable and sooner or later it's gonna be exposed, but for now I'll play nice.

MAY 2020
Time: 5:05 P.M.
Song - Lil Uzi Very
That way

Shit is Getting Real!!

April 3

Delaware - 393, 12 Death
PA - 7,264 - 90 Death
NJ - 25,590 - 537 Death

April 12

New Jersey - 58,151 / 2,183 Death
Delaware - 1,326 / 32 Death
PA - 6,152 / 160 Death

May 28

PA - 21,975 / 1,248 Death
NJ - 159,608 / 11,634
Delaware - 11, 401

Date: Jan 2021
Time: 8:41 P.M
Song: Lemonade
Don

January MADness!!

Donald Trump started a riot that took over the capital, now that he's has a few days left, they tryna impeach him (so sad) All White Nation, but if they were black tryna take over we've been treated very differently, football season is almost over, so now i have to find a new hobby to do on Sundays, Biden is filling neighborhoods up with the vaccine shot so that's good, haven't heard from destiny in a while hope she's okay.

Part 2

Jan 21, Time: 9:52 p.m
Mood: Cool
Song: Monica
What hurt the Most

So the baby is doing ok he/she is getting big, I'm still working Lovely is still doing online schooling I'm so over this shit, I need some time to myself, (omg) Love bug birthday is in 2 months (who's coming over) million dollar? Nobody different over the years as I look over things and all the things that I'm used to I'm not seeing (is that too much to ask) lack of attention is a mother fucker, it can take you to a place of darkness and full of hatred, "only the strong survive" will help you through it (if you allow them to help) but until then you reveal the ill, the only thing that's on my mind is me myself and I. "now that" I will never see that in her eyes. I love her so much, I can't see myself without her (she is all I have) the big 6 wow this girl is getting up there, I can live with that many more to come.

Feb 2021
Time: 10:30 P.M
Song: T.L.C. Hands up
Theme: Starting off right

I just upgraded from the note 10 to the iPhone 12 mini ☺ how fly is that for a bitch, I gotta stay top of the line (bitch's hattin hard) oh well I said I was gonna get it and I got it, destiny is having a boy so Sheed is gonna be hype (me too) paid my rent for the month, I feel good about that, pay the electric & gas on time, I like my little Phone, Lovely love it more doe, it's snowing outside and it wasn't no work for me so that was good, Lovely still in class, I can't wait until it's over, it's really messing up my sleep time, Mr Dennis he cool I like him, he be working with us. We are getting cable in a couple of days plus internet so this should be interesting. Love day is coming up hopefully the snow is gone by then but if not it will be just another work day, besides that How's Tami been doing...um not so damn bad, she's losing weight again but her friends are making her happy, she listen to Michael Jackson every chance she gets and the rest of her old school jams she likes to listen to, she puts family first (no matter what) she has a walk of extinction, the fellas fall for her, her smile could bring any darkness to light (she knows) And what does she do about it....Uses it to her advantage without anyone getting hurt. The darkness that she carries with her is a drug that she can't control. It's what makes her who she is (without the strength, power and will) an average common girl wouldn't be able to understand me. But who is she so many people want to know?? But with her...once you get close there's no turning back your lock in for life (but who would want to turn around from her. I'm damn sure wouldn't (that girl is one of a kind) her parents did a very good job of raising her. Thank you for that

Feb 2021
Time: 9:41 A.M.
Song - Beanie
Sigel - was the name

Love meltdown

So all month it's been snowing, raining, hailing and windy, destiny's stomach is growing, Holli thinking of ways to cheat the system once again, nu-nu and treasure going back and forth at camac st. Mellah keeps bugging me for money to feed other people. Sheed keeps drinking his life away, pop getting camac st. fixing up, nae got her car towed parking in a loading zone but she got it back. Oc had to curse Darren out for mooching around in my crib, so who knows if he coming back (don't care) it was a crazy shooting at Broad + olney, 7 people got shot so now the kool kids on the block is hiding out, still trying to make plans for lovely birthday she gonna be a big 7 I love her to death, gorgeous still being bad eating up everything, they cleaned out Holli apartment the mirror is the only thing left, Destiny went M.I.A, for some reason I still keeping the apartment together, spring is slow coming along I'm ready to take my braids out

April 2021
Time: 12:10 A.M.
Song - Kevin gates
Big Gangsta
Theme: Taking it day by day!

I'm still alive during this madness that is going on in this world right now, Lovely turned 7, she had an awesome birthday, I'll be 31 on Sunday, I got my 3rd tat yesterday I love it, it's expresses what I am and my meaning to this world, so for the ones I had showed they was feeling it, "the family" they doing well and fine, I'm still in my apartment, still working, paying my bills on time, making sure the House is warm in the winter, making sure she sees Mr. Dennis in the morning, keeps clean laundry, cooks meals, tolerates the bullshit, keeps our child safe and puts food on the table when he can't, helps with homework, he teaches lovely about the streets of life all for what??? To think about giving it all up every morning when I open my eyes. I do all these things to impress the person that I'm really ain't. I scream out for help all the time, even cried it out, but no one listened. I just don't get what I have to do for anybody to look my way (It doesn't even matter) because they stopped looking 17 yrs ago. Now, the woman that I had become now, boy I tell you, she aint nothing to be played with, she'll kill your soul before you know it. The spot lights are always on her so she never misses a shot, my shorty dew never misses a beat, "one act of kindness" that all it takes for a girl like me to take you to anywhere you need to go. I haven't talked to destiny in a while. I hope she is ok and the baby, the girl Tasha said she was in the area a couple days ago but she never moved the van.

April 2021
Time: 2:23 A.M
Song - Lovis gold
Quarantine Bae
Mood - Mellow

My favorite TV shows are.

Blue Bloods - They rock out for each other, even though it can get messy, But I love that they have Sunday dinner with each other and discuss it over food.

Chicago P.D - the whole team make sacrifices to save people lives, no man left behind.

Hawaii Five - o - Steve Mcfarret and Danny Williams, they are funny together but they make a perfect team, the water and the weather looks so beautiful out there.

Law and order - Detective Olivia, that's my bitch, she don't play no fucking games when it come to her cases, Detective Elliot stabler, he be snapping out to, but that's my bitch.

Ncis Los Angeles - Agent Kensi and Detective Deeks (omg-I love them to together) I'm so glad that the show made them hook up and get together and get married, she got into a bad airplane crash and paralyze her legs, I was crying over it (big baby) LL cool j, he be chilling in his car.

April 2021
Time:
Song: Ashanti - I'm not scared!
Theme: Fear

Over Turn it!

As I was growing up, I've seen a lot of violence in my life time, even though I've never been physical harm, I've allowed it to put fear in my heart, (will that be me one day) pretty girls cry every day - I don't wear no makeup, i get nervous when a 16 wheeler drives besides me, my heart panics when it's bad weather - never been in a car accident - can't enjoy roller coasters once it get to a certain height, it's over...my brain is telling me different, you got this, it's not hard, what's the problem? Million dollar? That's what got my heart so worry, my parents were speed demons when they were high, but never hit nobody so they musta was been driving right, I don't like carrying this heavy weight on me without knowing the cause, it's really a bad, the crazy thing about it is, I will jump over little things.

May 2021
Time: 11:52 P.M.
Song: Pooh Shiesty
Monday to Sunday

This school year is slowly ending up and I'm so happy, lovey is not failing in her classes (thanks to me) just a little bit more to go and we both can sleep on the same schedule they are starting to open the world up back up, we can start doing more things in the summer (the family doing good), the Honda Pilot had to go in the shop so we got a rental, a Nissan kick (foreign car) Holli he doing ok the cops not showing up for the gun and drug case, and Jantell case is on the first. C-ellie might be looking at adopting, destiny is keeping us in the dark on the pregnancy but I believe she is doing good, I'm just taking it day by day the summer is gonna get hot and more madness is bound to come, just keep it away from me and mines.

www.ingramcontent.com/pod-product-compliance
Lightning Source LLC
Chambersburg PA
CBHW032149040426
42449CB00005B/459